Contents

Sounds in this book

cl cr fl fr ft nd nk nt pl st

a (past, aircraft) a-e (plane) all (called)

ay (today) ea (reach) ie (flies) i-e (bike)

oa (road) o-e (nose) ou (about)

ow (arrows) y (sky)

Aircraft in the past

When we think about aircraft, we think about planes. But some aircraft long ago were not planes at all!

This hot air balloon was made hundreds of years ago.

A glider from long ago

This is an airship.

Planes in the past

This plane from long ago was called the Flyer.
It was made of wood, cloth and bits of bike!

It took off into the sky in 1903.
But the flight was over in seconds!

Planes today

Today, planes are made of metal. They are much bigger and fly faster than the Flyer.

These people are off on holiday.

Some planes are made to carry people.
Some are made to carry cargo.

Loading up with cargo

Runways

Lots of planes need a long runway to take off and land safely.

Planes must reach a high speed in order to take off.

But this fighter plane has no need
of a runway.
It can take off and land on a ship!

Helicopters

Helicopters do not need a runway. They can take off and land on a road – or a roof!

rotor blades

Helicopters can save lives!

This aircraft takes off like a helicopter but it flies like a plane!

Stunt planes

Some people like to fly just for fun.
Some of them can do stunts —
like a loop-the-loop.

The plane is
upside down!

Some people fly in display teams,
like the Red Arrows.
The stunts are very tricky to do!

Parts of a plane

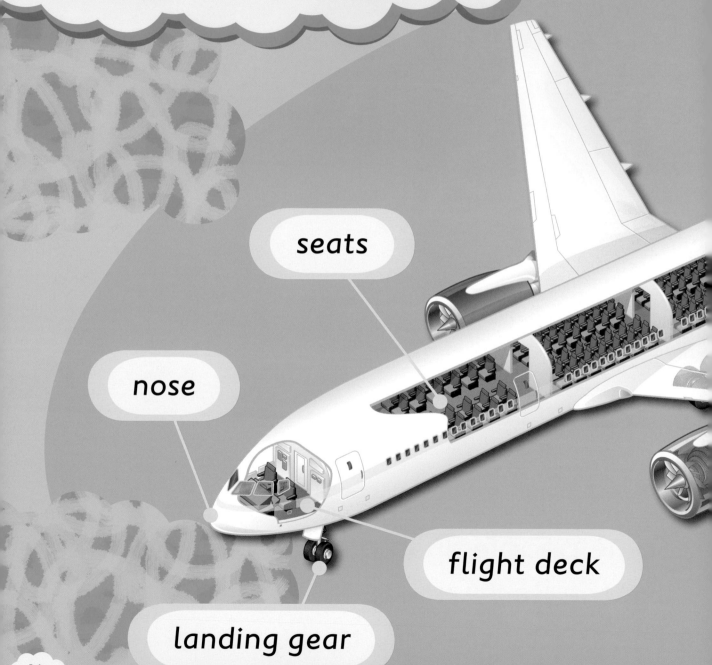

seats

nose

flight deck

landing gear

Index